# YCT

## 标准教程
STANDARD COURSE

## 活动手册 1
ACTIVITY BOOK

主编　苏英霞
Lead Author　Su Yingxia

编者　王蕾　蔡楠
Authors　Wang Lei　Cai Nan

高等教育出版社·北京

# 目录 Content

**Lesson 1** 你好！Hello! .................................................. 1

**Lesson 2** 你叫什么？What's your name? .......................... 5

**Lesson 3** 他是谁？Who is he? ..................................... 9

**Lesson 4** 我家有四口人。There are four people in my family ...... 13

**Lesson 5** 我6岁。I'm 6 years old. ................................ 17

**Lesson 6** 你的个子真高！You're so tall! ......................... 21

**Lesson 7** 这是谁的狗？Whose dog is this? ....................... 25

**Lesson 8** 我去商店。I'm going to the store. ..................... 29

**Lesson 9** 今天星期几？What day is it today? .................... 33

**Lesson 10** 现在几点？What time is it? ............................ 37

**Lesson 11** 你吃什么？What would you like to eat? ............... 41

参考答案 Answers .................................................... 45

# Lesson 1

## 你好!
Hello!

**1 描一描。** Trace over the Pinyin and characters.

| 1 | 2 | 3 | 4 | 5 | 6 | 7 | 8 | 9 | 10 |
|---|---|---|---|---|---|---|---|---|---|
| yī | èr | sān | sì | wǔ | liù | qī | bā | jiǔ | shí |
| 一 | 二 | 三 | 四 | 五 | 六 | 七 | 八 | 九 | 十 |

**2 连一连。** Match the Pinyin with pictures.

yī　èr　sān　sì　wǔ　liù　qī　bā　jiǔ　shí

**3** 起名字。Give yourself a Chinese name.

在老师的帮助下，给自己起一个汉语名字，并做一个漂亮的名签吧。With the help of your teacher, come up with a Chinese name for yourself, then make yourself a pretty name badge.

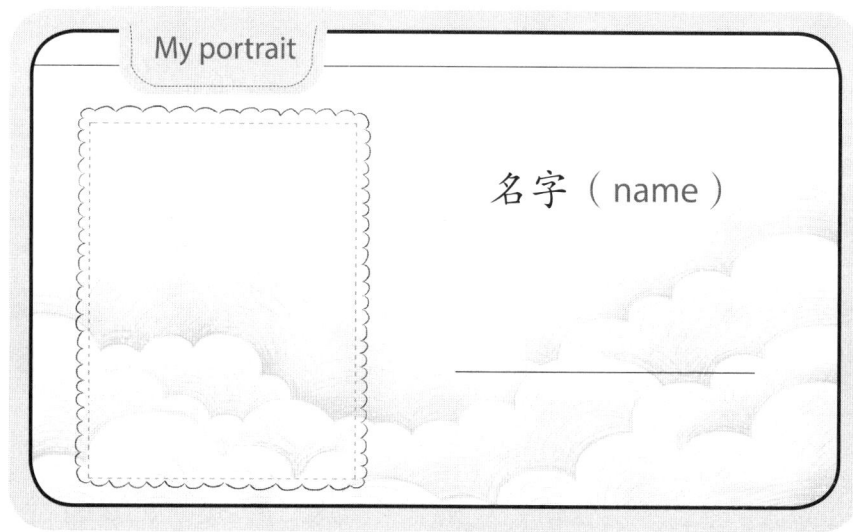

**4** 说一说。Let's talk.

每人举着自己的名签，轮流跟同学们打招呼，然后说再见。Holding up your name badges, take it in turns to greet and say goodbye to everyone.

你好！
Hello!

**5** **涂颜色。** Color the numbers in.

给数字相同的部分涂上一样的颜色，画出一只可爱的蝴蝶。 Color in the cute picture of a butterfly by coloring each segment according to the numbers.

## 6 我的小书。 My Chinese number book.

数一数，粘一粘。 Count the pictures, then cut out the numbers and stick them in the right box.

| yī | èr | sān | sì | wǔ |
|---|---|---|---|---|
| 一 | 二 | 三 | 四 | 五 |
| liù | qī | bā | jiǔ | shí |
| 六 | 七 | 八 | 九 | 十 |

# 你叫什么?
## What's your name?

**1** 找一找，连一连。 Help the dog out by finding and connecting all the phrases "很高兴".

↓ 入口 Entrance

| 很 | 高兴 | 不 | 认识 | 我 |
| 好 | 很 | 什么 | 好 | 她 |
| 不 | 高兴 | 很 | 高兴 | 认识 |
| 认识 | 你 | 叫 | 很 | 高兴 |
| 老师 | 不 | 她 | 认识 | 很 |
| 她 | 很 | 老师 | 我 | 高兴 |

→ 出口 Exit

**2** 找一找，写一写。 Find the *Pinyin* by filling in the missing letters according to the shape keys below, then translate the Chinese words into English.

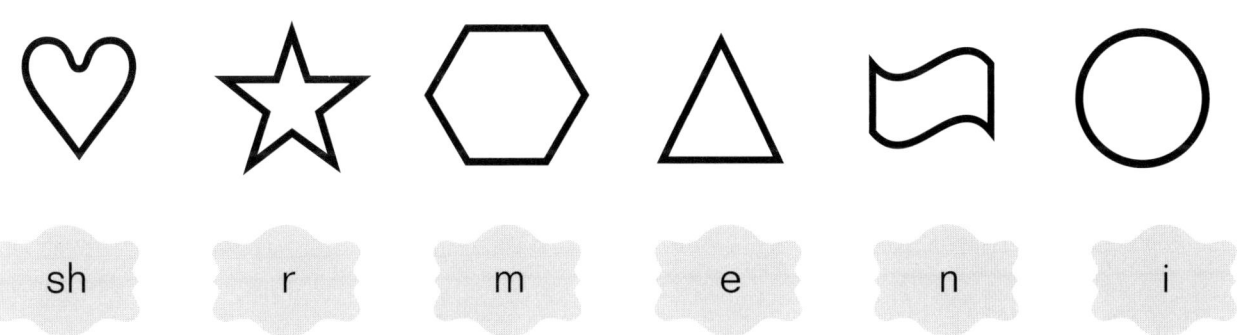

(1)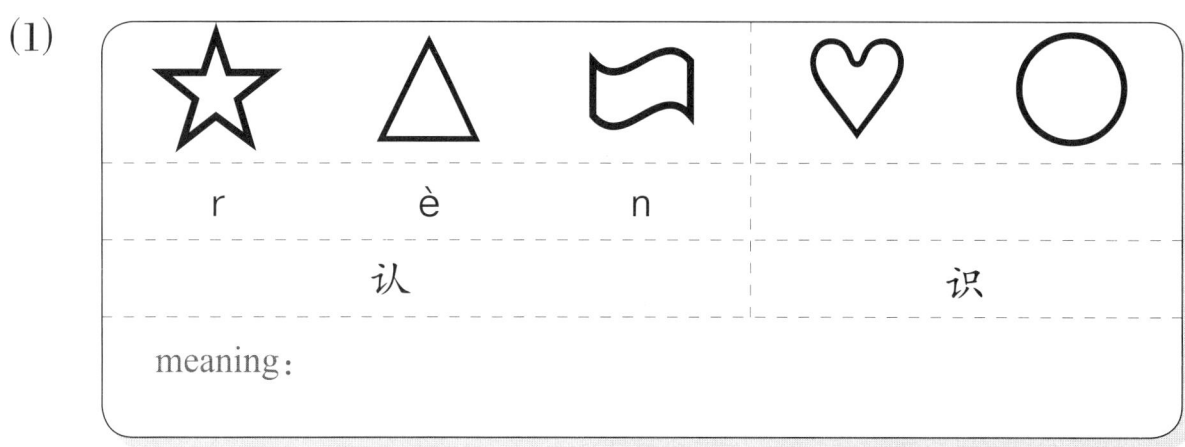

r è n

认　　　识

meaning:

(2)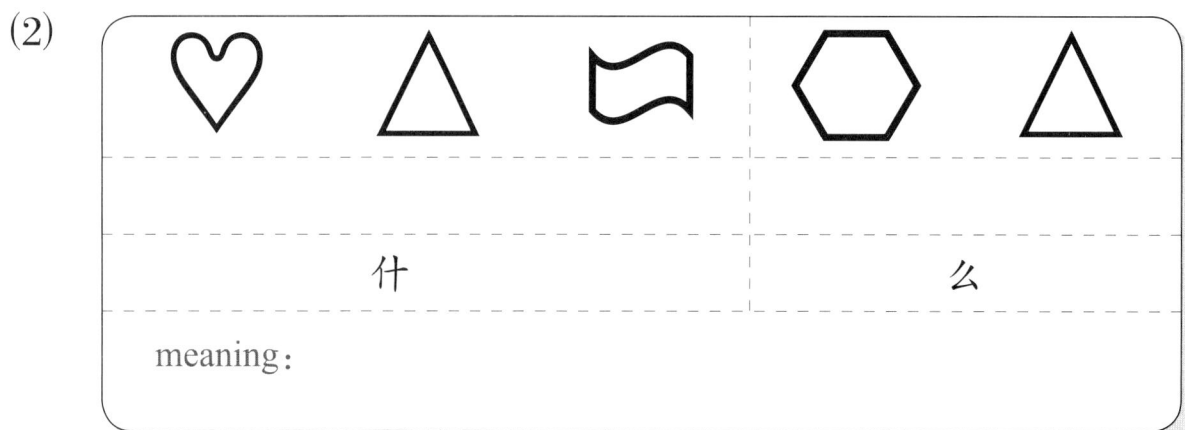

什　　　么

meaning:

**3** 看一看，选一选。Look at the pictures and choose the appropriate word for each picture.

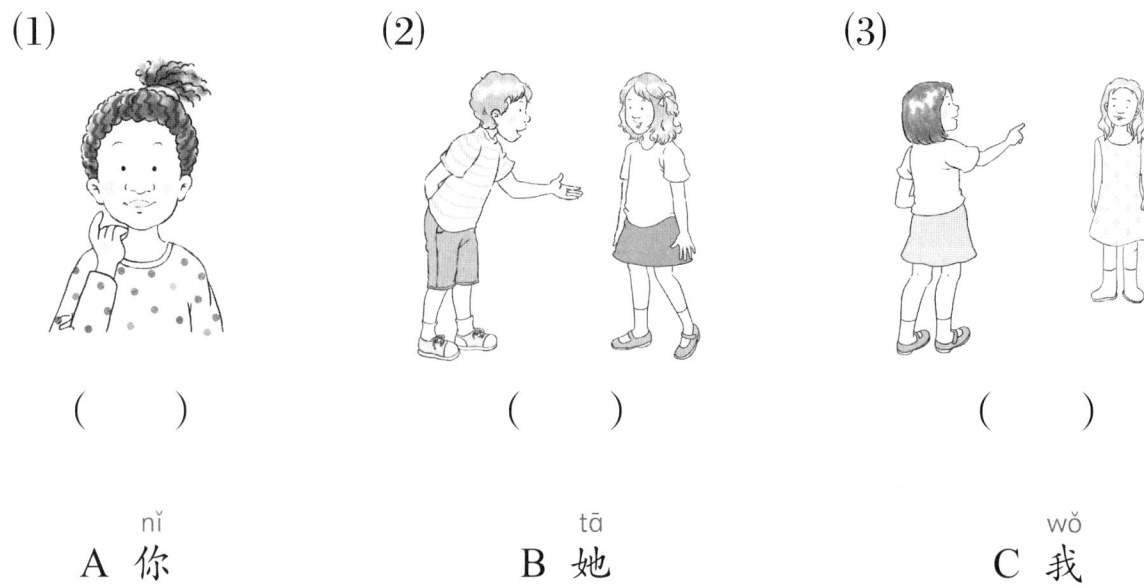

(1) (　　)  (2) (　　)  (3) (　　)

A 你 (nǐ)　　B 她 (tā)　　C 我 (wǒ)

你叫什么？
What's your name?

2

**4** 读一读，涂一涂。Read the phrases below and color in the right pictures.

hěn hǎo
(1) 很 好

A        B

bù hǎo
(2) 不 好

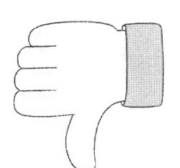

A        B

bù gāoxìng
(3) 不 高兴

A        B

hěn gāoxìng
(4) 很 高兴

A        B

**5** 看一看，说一说。Have conversations with your partner using the pictures and examples below.

Nǐ rènshi tā / tā ma?
A：你认识他／她吗？
Bú rènshi.
B：不认识。

Nǐ rènshi tā / tā ma?
A：你认识他／她吗？
Rènshi.
B：认识。
Tā / tā jiào shénme?
A：他／她叫什么？
Tā / tā jiào…
B：他／她叫……

7

**6** 画一画，说一说。 Draw a picture of a cartoon character, your friend or yourself, then introduce them to your partner in Chinese.

例：你好！我叫_____。认识你很高兴！
（Nǐ hǎo! Wǒ jiào _____. Rènshi nǐ hěn gāoxìng!）

# Lesson 3 他是谁？
## Who is he?

**1 小猫钓鱼。** Match the characters with the Pinyin by helping the cats catch the right fish.

**2 抱作一团。** Group hug.

每个学生拿一张汉字卡片。老师说一个句子，手拿这些卡片的同学要迅速抱在一起，并大声读出该句子。Each student takes one of the character cards. As the teacher reads out a sentence, students holding those characters get together in a huddle, and then shout out the sentence.

| tā | shì | shéi | nǎ | guó |
|---|---|---|---|---|
| 他 | 是 | 谁 | 哪 | 国 |
| rén | zhōng | jiào | chéng | lóng |
| 人 | 中 | 叫 | 成 | 龙 |

9

**3** 连一连。Match the pictures with their countries.

**4** 根据图片完成对话。Complete the conversations according to the pictures.

例：A: Tā / tā shì shéi?
他 / 她是谁？

B: _____。

A: Tā / tā shì nǎ guó rén?
他 / 她是哪国人？

B: _____。

# 他是谁？ 3
Who is he?

**5** **找朋友。** Find your friends.

每个学生拿一张卡片。用下面的句型找到和你同国籍的朋友。Each student takes one of the cards below. Use the sentence patterns to find classmates who are the same nationality as yourself.

Jīn Xiùzhēn　Hánguórén
金秀珍　韩国人

Mǎlì　Jiānádàrén
玛丽　加拿大人

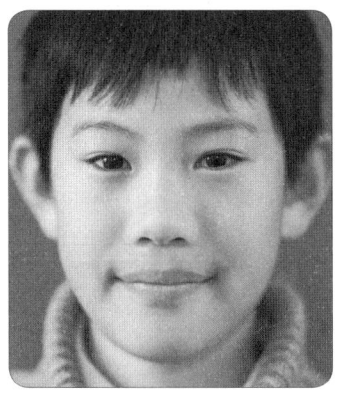

Lǐ Qiáng　Zhōngguórén
李强　中国人

Mǎdīng　Yīngguórén
马丁　英国人

Shānběn Àiměi　Rìběnrén
山本爱美　日本人

Dānní'ěr　Měiguórén
丹尼尔　美国人

Nǐ hǎo,
你好，
nǐ jiào shénme?
你叫什么？

Nǐ shì nǎ guó rén?
你是哪国人？

Rènshi nǐ hěn gāoxìng.
认识你很高兴。

Wǒ jiào ___.
我叫＿＿。

Wǒ shì ___ rén.
我是＿＿人。

Rènshi nǐ wǒ yě hěn gāoxìng.
认识你我也很高兴？

**6** 选词填空。Fill in the blanks with the words in the box.

| | nǎ | dōu | shéi | piàoliang | rènshi |
|---|---|---|---|---|---|
| | A 哪 | B 都 | C 谁 | D 漂亮 | E 认识 |

(1) Tā shì Měiguórén, wǒ shì Měiguórén, wǒmen _____ shì Měiguórén.
她是美国人，我是美国人，我们_____是美国人。

(2) Wǒ māma hěn _____.
我妈妈很_____。

(3) Wǒ bù _____ tā. Tā shì _____?
我不_____她。她是_____?

(4) Nǐ shì _____ guó rén?
你是_____国人?

**7** 名片设计。Design your own name card and stick it on your locker.

★ 国旗要有创意。Draw your national flag in a creative way.

# Lesson 4

## 我家有四口人。
There are four people in my family.

**1** 数一数，有几个？ Count all the characters and say how many there are of each.

| 哥 | 哥 | 有 | 妈 | 姐 | 爸 |
|---|---|---|---|---|---|
| 几 | 姐 | 姐 | 妈 | 姐 | 爸 |
| 妈 | 妈 | 爸 | 爸 | 没 | 有 |
| 妹 | 口 | 和 | 姐 | 姐 | 个 |
| 妹 | 爸 | 爸 | 家 | 口 | 哥 |
| 妈 | 妈 | 个 | 妈 | 妈 | 哥 |

bàba
爸爸 father _____ 个

māma
妈妈 mother _____ 个

gēge
哥哥 big brother _____ 个

jiějie
姐姐 big sister _____ 个

mèimei
妹妹 little sister _____ 个

**2** 写拼音，说一说我的家人。 Write the *Pinyin* and talk about my family.

**3** 写一写，读一读。Complete the sentences and read out.

写出你自己、家人和好朋友的名字，然后在班级里大声读出来。Write down the names of yourself, your family members and friends to finish the sentences, then read them out loud to the class.

(1) Wǒ jiào
我叫_____。
My name is _____.

(2) Wǒ gēge / dìdi jiào
我哥哥/弟弟叫_____。
My brother's name is _____.

(3) Wǒ jiějie / mèimei jiào
我姐姐/妹妹叫_____。
My sister's name is _____.

(4) Wǒ hǎo péngyou jiào
我好朋友叫_____。
My best friend's name is _____.

**4** 小调查：你的家。Class survey: about your family.

| tóngxué míngzi<br>同学名字 | gēge<br>哥哥 | jiějie<br>姐姐 | dìdi<br>弟弟 | mèimei<br>妹妹 |
|---|---|---|---|---|
| 1 | | | | |
| 2 | | | | |
| 3 | | | | |
| 4 | | | | |
| 5 | | | | |

Q: Nǐ yǒu gēge ( jiějie / dìdi / mèimei ) ma?
你有哥哥（姐姐/弟弟/妹妹）吗?

A: Yǒu / méiyǒu.
有/没有。

Q: Yǒu jǐ ge?
有几个?

A: Yǒu _____ ge.
有_____个。

14

# 4

## 我家有四口人。
There are four people in my family.

**5** 大富翁游戏。 Chinese Monopoly.

两人一组，轮流掷骰子。先用汉语说出骰子的点数，然后回答大富翁棋盘上的问题。In pairs, take it in turns to roll the dice. Read out the number on the dice in Chinese, then answer the question on the Monopoly board.

⑧ Nǐ rènshi Chéng Lóng ma? 你认识成龙吗?

⑨ Chéng Lóng shì nǎ guó rén? 成龙是哪国人?

⑩ Nǐ shì nǎ guó rén? 你是哪国人?

⑪ Nǐ jiā yǒu jǐ kǒu rén? 你家有几口人?

⑫ Nǐ yǒu gēge ma? 你有哥哥吗?

⑬ Nǐ yǒu jǐ ge jiějie? 你有几个姐姐?

⑦ chūjú 出局 (Out)

⑰ Nǐ de lǎoshī jiào shénme? 你的老师叫什么?

⑯ Nǐ hǎo péngyou jiào shénme? 你好朋友叫什么?

⑮ How do you say "two little sisters"?

⑭ chūjú 出局 (Out)

Win!

⑥ Rènshi nǐ hěn gāoxìng! 认识你很高兴!

⑤ Nǐ jiào shénme? 你叫什么?

④ Make gestures from one to ten.

③ Count from one to ten in Chinese.

② Zàijiàn! 再见!

① Nǐ hǎo! 你好!

Start!

15

**6** 抽卡片游戏。Card game.

两人一组，每人手持一套卡片。互相抽对方的卡片，抽中相同的就放到一边，不同的留在手里。谁手里的卡片先抽完，谁获胜。In pairs, each student holds a set of cards. Players take a card from each other's hand simultaneously. Any new pairs of matching cards are put away, while non-matching cards are kept in hand. The first player to get rid of all the cards in the hand is the winner.

| bàba 爸爸 | māma 妈妈 | gēge 哥哥 | jiějie 姐姐 |
| mèimei 妹妹 | jiā 家 | yǒu 有 | jǐ 几 |
| kǒu 口 | hé 和 | méiyǒu 没有 | gè 个 |
| tā 他 | shì 是 | lǎoshī 老师 | hǎo 好 |
| hěn 很 | nǐ 你 | tā 她 | wǒ 我 |

# Lesson 5  我6岁。
I'm 6 years old.

**1** 找一找，连一连。Find and match the characters.

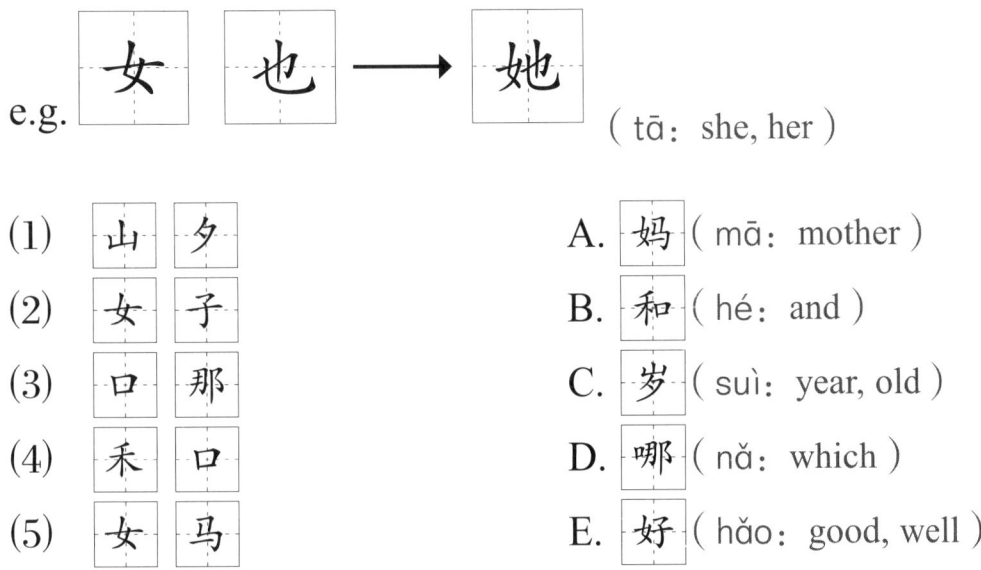

**2** 找一找，涂一涂。Find and color in the apples which correspond to the words in the sentences below (using the same color as they appear in the sentences), then read the sentences out loud.

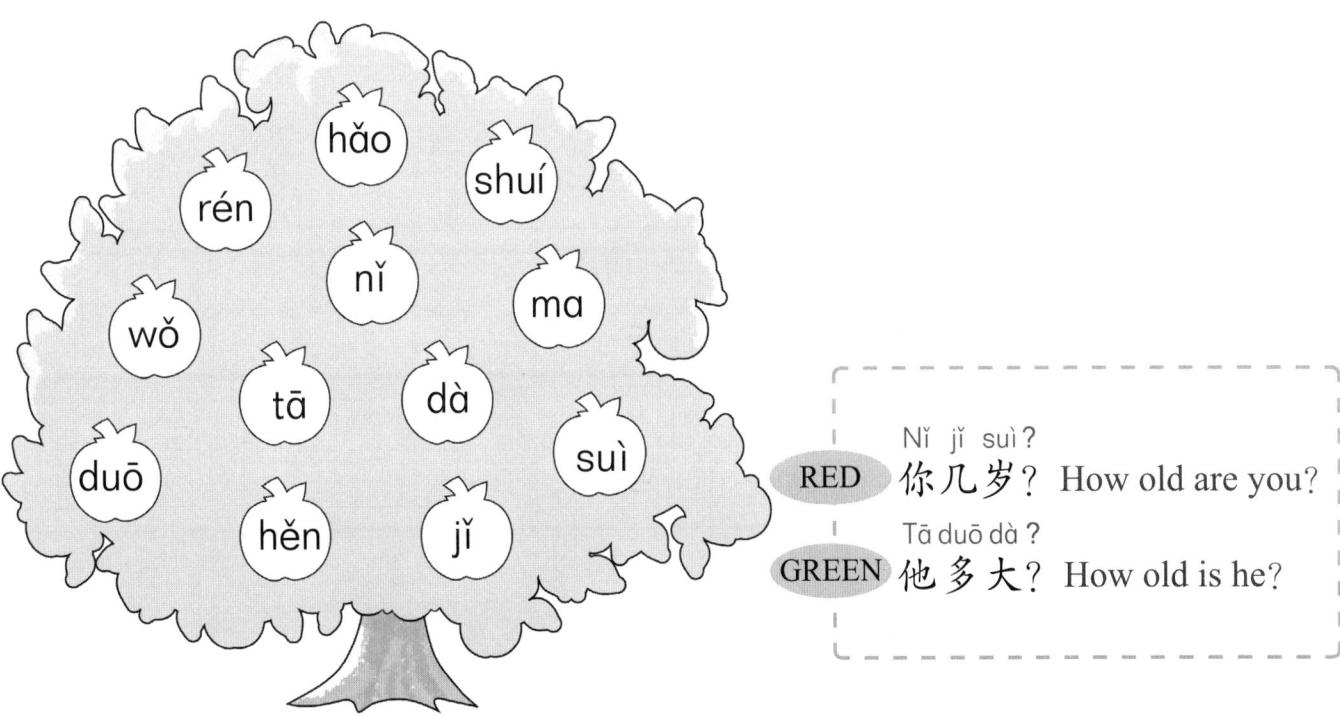

**3** 写一写，读一读。 Use the conversion table below to fill in the gaps with either Arabic or Chinese numbers, then read them out loud.

| 1 | 2 | 3 | 4 | 5 | 6 | 7 | 8 | 9 | 10 |
|---|---|---|---|---|---|---|---|---|---|
| yī | èr | sān | sì | wǔ | liù | qī | bā | jiǔ | shí |
| 一 | 二 | 三 | 四 | 五 | 六 | 七 | 八 | 九 | 十 |

(1) 八 → _____  (2) 十 → _____

(3) 十五 → _____  (4) 二十三 → _____

(5) 1 → _____  (6) 3 → _____

(7) 20 → _____  (8) 81 → _____

**4** 算一算，写一写。 Work out the sum and write the answer in Chinese characters.

(1) 六 − 三 = ☐

(2) 十 − 九 = ☐

(3) 二 + 七 = ☐

(4) 六 + 四 = ☐

我6岁。
I'm 6 years old.

# 5

**5** 想一想，写一写。Answer the questions by filling in the gaps.

(1) A：你几岁？
    B：我＿＿＿＿岁。

(2) A：你家有几口人？
    B：我家有＿＿＿＿口人。

(3) A：你有几个老师？
    B：我有＿＿＿＿个老师。

(4) A：你认识几个中国人？
    B：＿＿＿＿个。

**6** 看一看，说一说。Work out the ages of the people in the pictures below, then say how old they are in Chinese.

Name: Cindy Smith
Date of Birth: August 4, 2013

Name: Mary Smith
Date of Birth: June 11, 2011

妹妹＿＿＿＿岁，姐姐＿＿＿＿岁。

**7** 问一问，填一填。Complete the questionnaire by asking your classmates questions in Chinese.

|   | Name | Nationality | Age | Number of family members |
|---|---|---|---|---|
| 1 | | | | |
| 2 | | | | |
| 3 | | | | |
| 4 | | | | |
| 5 | | | | |

**8** 和父母一起做。With your parents, go online and find out the ages of the following people/characters.

(1) 米老鼠（Mickey Mouse）＿＿＿＿岁。
　　Mǐlǎoshǔ　　　　　　　　　　suì

(2) 芭比（Barbie Millicent Roberts）＿＿＿＿岁。
　　Bābǐ　　　　　　　　　　　　suì

(3) 加菲猫（Garfield）＿＿＿＿岁。
　　Jiāfēimāo　　　　　　suì

(4) 总统（president）＿＿＿＿岁。
　　Zǒngtǒng　　　　　　suì

(5) 爸爸＿＿＿＿岁，妈妈＿＿＿＿岁。
　　Bàba　　suì　　māma　　suì

(6) Name of your idol ＿＿＿＿, his/her age ＿＿＿＿.

# Lesson 6 — 你的个子真高!
## You're so tall!

**1** 宾果。Bingo.

老师读5个生词"你""的""鼻子""真""长",最先把5个连成一条直线的学生获胜。The teacher reads out a sentence with 5 new words. The first student to find and connect the 5 words in a straight line is the winner.

| cháng | dà | nǐ | gèzi | nǐ |
|---|---|---|---|---|
| dà | zhēn | de | de | shǒu |
| gāo | gāo | bízi | tóufa | xiǎo |
| ěrduo | zhēn | zhēn | de | bízi |
| cháng | xiǎo | cháng | yǎnjing | nì |

**2** 说一说。Say the parts of the body in Chinese.

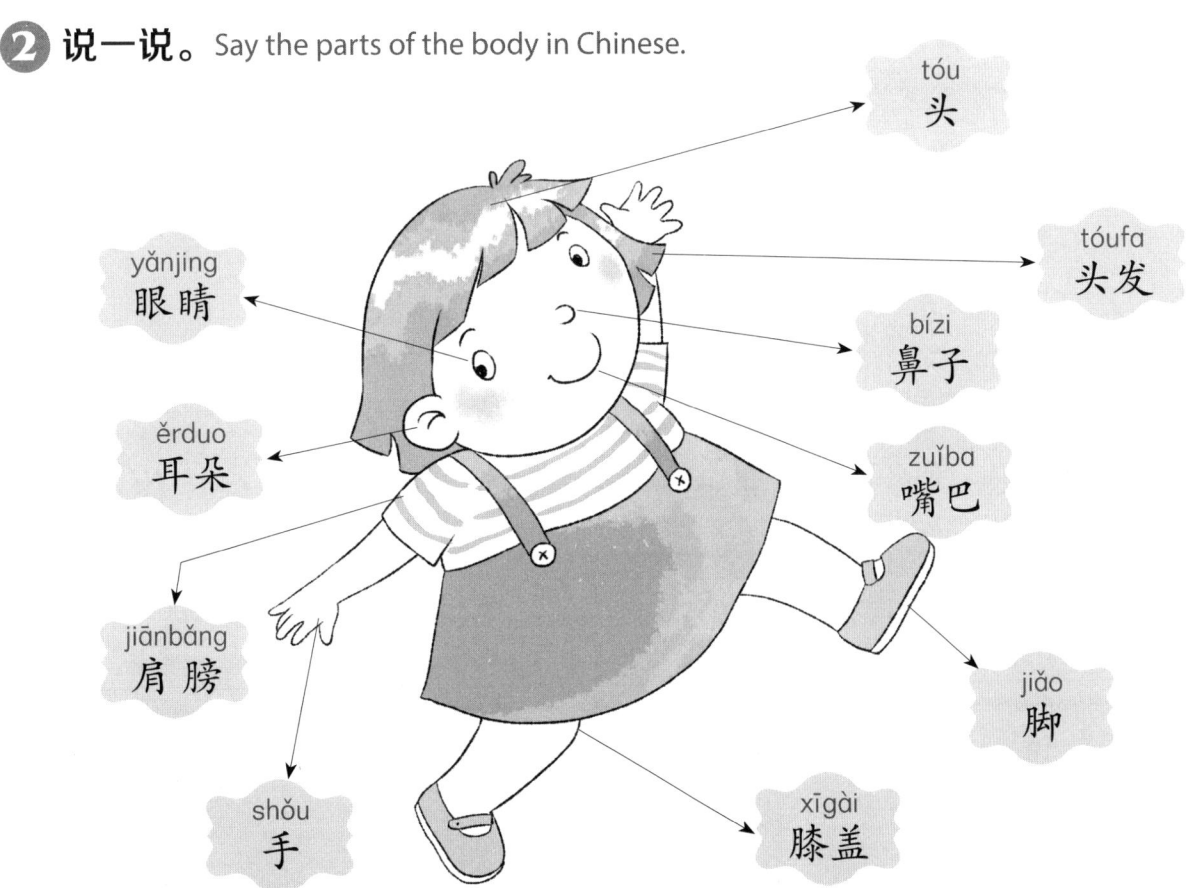

tóu 头
tóufa 头发
bízi 鼻子
zuǐba 嘴巴
jiǎo 脚
xīgài 膝盖
shǒu 手
jiānbǎng 肩膀
ěrduo 耳朵
yǎnjing 眼睛

**3** 汉字炸弹。Chinese character bombs.

3—4人一组，依次从盒子里抽卡片（有字的一面朝下），读出生词。说对的自己留下，说错的放回盒子，抽到炸弹要把手里的卡片全部放回去。最后手里卡片最多的获胜。In groups of 3 or 4, take it in turns to take a word card from the box (with the words face down), then read the word aloud. If you say it correctly you can keep the card; if you read it wrong, the card goes back in the box; if you get a bomb card, all your cards must go back in the box. Whoever has the most cards at the end is the winner.

| tóufa<br>头发 | bízi<br>鼻子 | yǎnjing<br>眼睛 | ěrduo<br>耳朵 |
|---|---|---|---|
| shǒu<br>手 | de<br>的 | xiǎo<br>小 | dà<br>大 |
| cháng<br>长 | gèzi<br>个子 | zhēn<br>真 | gāo<br>高 |
| mèimei<br>妹妹 | hěn<br>很 | bù<br>不 | nǐ<br>你 |
| shéi<br>谁 | tóu<br>头 | 💣 | 💣 |

# 6 你的个人子真高！
You're so tall!

**4** 连一连。 Match the pictures with the sentences.

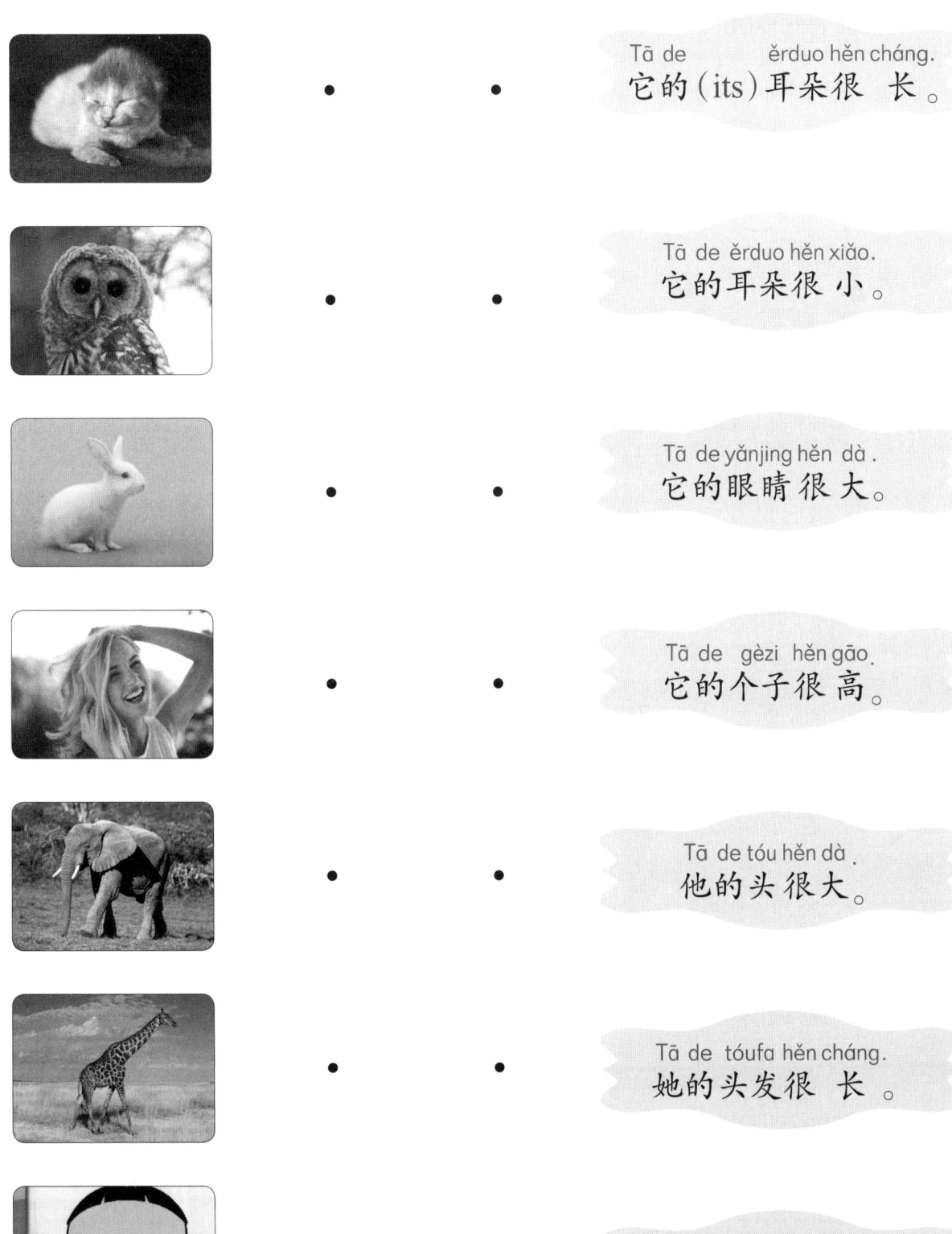

**5** 读一读，画一画，说一说。Let's read, draw and write.

画一个自己喜欢的动物，然后仿照例子介绍一下它。Draw a picture of your favorite animal, then introduce it to everyone using the example below for reference.

例：
Nǐ hǎo, tā jiào Nini. Tā wǔ suì.
你好，它叫Nini。它5岁。
Tā de yǎnjing hěn dà. Tā de bízi hěn xiǎo.
它的眼睛很大。它的鼻子很小。
Tā de wěiba hěn cháng.
它的尾巴很长。

# Lesson 7 这是谁的狗？
## Whose dog is this?

**❶ 选一选。** Choose the correct character to complete the sentence.

(1) Zhè shì wǒ de ___。
 This is my cat.
 A 猫 (māo)　B 狸 (lí)　C 猪 (zhū)

(2) Nà shì wǒ de ___。
 That is my dog.
 A 苟 (gǒu)　B 狗 (gǒu)　C 狐 (hú)

(3) Zhèr yǒu hěn duō xiǎo ___。
 There are lots of fish here.
 A 鲜 (xiān)　B 渔 (yú)　C 鱼 (yú)

(4) Nàr yǒu hěn duō xiǎo ___。
 There are lots of birds over there.
 A 乌 (wū)　B 鸟 (niǎo)　C 马 (mǎ)

**❷ 找一找，圈一圈。** Find out and circle the Pinyin in the table.

| m | l | n | i | a | o | y |
|---|---|---|---|---|---|---|
| a | m | z | i | n | g | u |
| o | c | h | k | a | n | x |
| x | q | g | o | u | g | j |
| u | i | a | o | z | h | e |
| n | a | o | u | d | u | o |

(1) māo（cat）
(2) gǒu（dog）
(3) yú（fish）
(4) niǎo（bird）
(5) zhè（this）
(6) nà（that）
(7) kàn（look）
(8) duō（many）

3 找一找，说一说。In pairs, find the owners of each animal, then take it in turns to ask and answer questions, as in the example below.

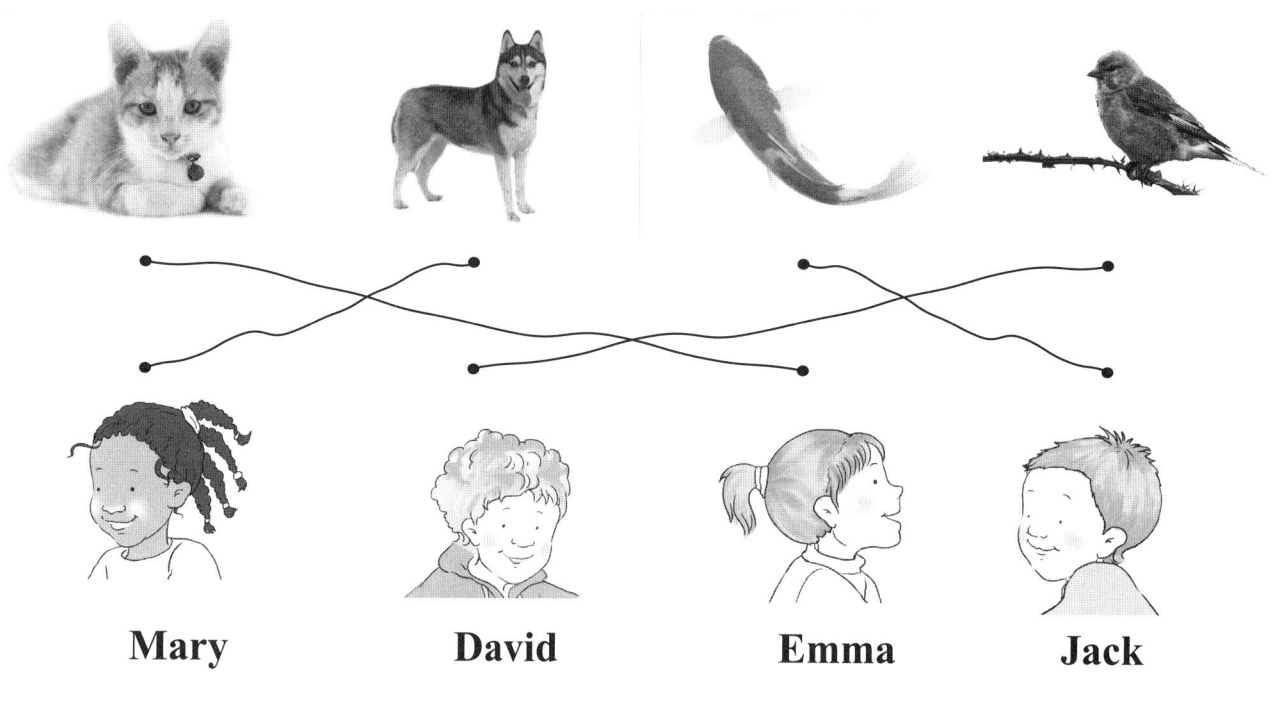

例：A：Zhè shì shéi de māo / gǒu / yú / niǎo?
　　　这 是 谁 的 猫 / 狗 / 鱼 / 鸟？

　　B：Zhè shì ___ de māo / gǒu / yú / niǎo.
　　　这 是 _____ 的 猫 / 狗 / 鱼 / 鸟。

4 填表格，说一说。Fill in the table below, then use it to make sentences about each of the animals and yourself.

|  | māo 猫 | gǒu 狗 | yú 鱼 | niǎo 鸟 | wǒ 我 |
|---|---|---|---|---|---|
| yǎnjing 眼睛 | ○ |  |  |  |  |
| ěrduo 耳朵 | ○ |  |  |  |  |
| bízi 鼻子 | ○ |  |  |  |  |
| shǒu 手 | × |  |  |  |  |

例：Māo yǒu yǎnjing, ěrduo hé bízi, méiyǒu shǒu.
　　猫 有 眼睛、耳朵 和 鼻子，没有 手。

# 7 这是谁的狗？
Whose dog is this?

**5** 两人一组，猜一猜。Work in pairs to guess the animals.

例： A： Zhè/nà shì shénme?
这/那是什么？

B： Zhè/nà shì
这/那是_____。

 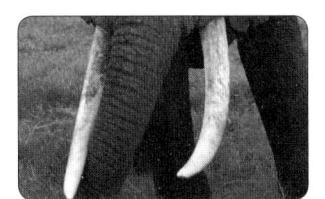 
 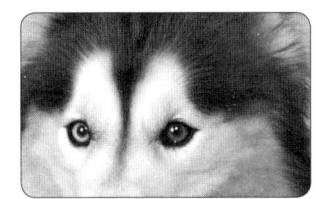 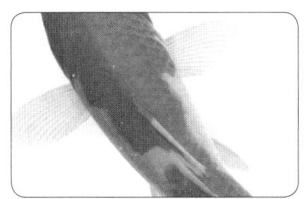
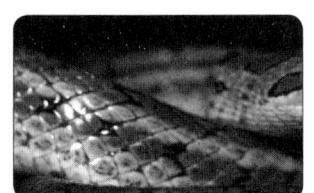  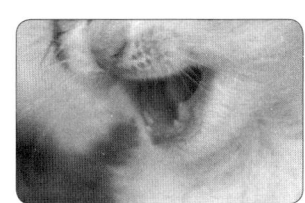

**6** 说说唱唱，然后在班里轮流表演。Learn the song and then take it in turns to perform for the class.

  　miāo　miāo　miāo

  　wāng　wāng　wāng

  　pū　pū　pū

  　jiū　jiū　jiū

**7** 猜一猜。Guess the word.

一个学生到教室前边,挑选一张词卡,文字向内放在胸前。其他学生用"那是……吗?"来提问。猜对的学生到前边继续这个活动。A student comes to the front of the class and chooses a word card, taking care to conceal the word from the rest of the class. The other students attempt to guess the word using Chinese. Whoever correctly guesses the word comes to the front and chooses another card.

★ 老师先用词卡带领全班复习一遍,再做游戏。

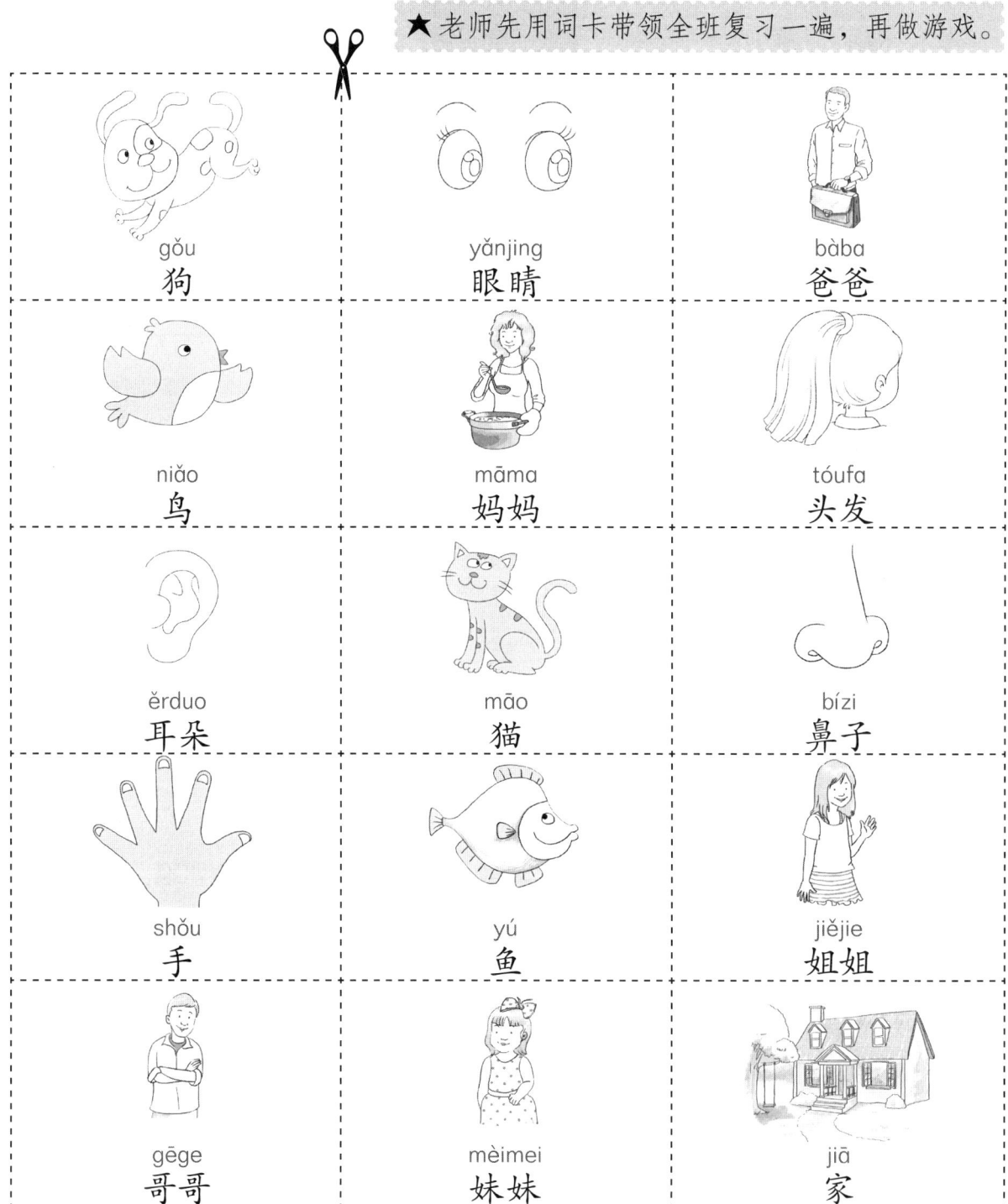

# Lesson 8

## 我去商店。
## I'm going to the store.

**1** 寻找爆米花。Find the right pieces of popcorn.

两人一组，根据爆米花桶上的汉字找到相应的拼音并朗读。In pairs, match the characters on the popcorn bucket with the corresponding *Pinyin* on the popcorn, then read out the words.

**2** 打电话。Make a phone call.

老师把自己家/好朋友的电话写在黑板上。学生轮流用教室里的电话或老师的手机练习打电话。The teacher writes his or her home phone number or a friend's number on the board. Students then take it in turns to use the teacher's phone to call the number and have a telephone conversation.

Nǐ hǎo, wǒ shì _____. lǎoshī zài jiā ma?
你好，我是_____。_____老师在家吗？

Tā / tā bú zài jiā, tā / tā zài xuéxiào.
他/她不在家，他/她在学校。

Xièxie, zàijiàn.
谢谢，再见。

Zàijiàn.
再见。

**3** 连一连。Match the sentences with the pictures.

Tā huí jiā.
他回家。

Tāmen qù xuéxiào.
他们去学校。

Tāmen qù Zhōngguó.
他们去中国。

Tā qù yīyuàn.
她去医院。

Wǒmen qù shāngdiàn.
我们去商店。

我去商店。
I'm going to the store.

**8**

**4** 小花粘在哪儿？Where is the small flower stuck?

两人一组完成句子，然后老师组织全班表演。Students work in pairs to complete the sentences before acting them out as a whole class.

(1)

Xuésheng： Xiǎo huā zhān zài nǎr ?
学 生 ： 小 花 粘 在 哪 儿 ?
Where is the small flower stuck?

Lǎoshī ： Zhān zài xiǎopéngyou de bízi shang.
老 师 ： 粘 在 小 朋 友 的 鼻 子 上 。
It's stuck on the noses.

(2)

Xuésheng： Xiǎo huā zhān ?
学 生 ： 小 花 粘 _____ ?

Lǎoshī ： Zhān zài xiǎopéngyou de shang.
老 师 ： 粘 在 小 朋 友 的 _____ 上 。

(3)

Xuésheng： Xiǎo huā zhān ?
学 生 ： 小 花 粘 _____ ?

Lǎoshī ： Zhān zài xiǎopéngyou de shang.
老 师 ： 粘 在 小 朋 友 的 _____ 上 。

(4)

Xuésheng： Xiǎo huā zhān ?
学 生 ： 小 花 粘 _____ ?

Lǎoshī ： Zhān zài xiǎopéngyou de xīgài shang.
老 师 ： 粘 在 小 朋 友 的 膝 盖 上 。

(5)

Xuésheng： Xiǎo huā zhān ?
学 生 ： 小 花 粘 _____ ?

Lǎoshī ： Zhān zài xiǎopéngyou de shang.
老 师 ： 粘 在 小 朋 友 的 _____ 上 。

**5** 读一读，写一写，画一画。Let's read, write and draw.

根据对话画画儿，把"去"字用不同颜色写在彩虹下面。Draw pictures according to the short sentences below, then write the character "去" underneath the rainbow in different colors.

(1) A：小狗去学校吗？
　　B：不去学校。

(2) A：小狗去商店吗？
　　B：不去商店。

(3) A：小狗回家吗？
　　B：不回家。

(4) A：小狗去哪儿？
　　B：去那儿！去那儿！

(1)

(2)

(3)

(4)

# Lesson 9 今天星期几？
## What day is it today?

**1** 找一找，连一连。 Match the characters with the corresponding pictographs.

**2** 读一读，找不同。 Read and find the different one in each group.

(1) yī 一　　sān 三　　tiān 天　　sì 四

(2) yuè 月　　hào 号　　jǐ 几　　xīngqī 星期

(3) jīntiān 今天　　xiǎo niǎo 小鸟　　Xīngqītiān 星期天　　míngtiān 明天

(4) xǐhuan 喜欢　　yǎnjing 眼睛　　ěrduo 耳朵　　bízi 鼻子

**3** 写一写，读一读。Complete the sequences, then read them out loud.

例：　qī yuè 7 月 → bā yuè 8 月 → jiǔ yuè 9 月

(1) sān yuè 3 月 → yuè ____月 → yuè ____月

(2) yuè ____月 → yuè ____月 → shí'èr yuè 12 月

(3) èr yuè shísān hào 2 月 13 号 → èr yuè ____ hào 2 月____号 → ____ yuè ____ hào ____月____号

(4) Xīngqī 星期____ → Xīngqī 星期____ → Xīngqī'èr 星期二

**4** 看谁填得快。Fill in the gaps in the dates below. Whoever gets all the answers correct first wins.

Your mother's birthday:

____月____号

New year's Day:

____月____号

Christmas eve:

____月____号

China's National Day:

____月____号

Mother' day of this year:

____月____号

Halloween of this year:

____月____号

# 今天星期几?
## What day is it today?

**9**

**5** 问一问，答一答。With a partner, practice asking and answering the following questions.

**A**

(1) Jīntiān jǐ yuè jǐ hào?
今天几月几号？

(2) Jīntiān Xīngqīsì.
今天星期四。

(3) Wǒ bā suì.
我8岁。

(4) Nǐ de shēngrì shì jǐ yuè jǐ hào?
你的生日是几月几号？

(5) Wǒ xǐhuan Xīngqītiān.
我喜欢星期天。

(6) Nǐ jiā yǒu jǐ kǒu rén?
你家有几口人？

**B**

A. Nǐ xǐhuan xīngqī jǐ?
你喜欢星期几？

B. Wǒ jiā yǒu wǔ kǒu rén.
我家有五口人。

C. Nǐ jǐ suì?
你几岁？

D. Wǒ de shēngrì shì èr yuè yī hào.
我的生日是2月1号。

E. Jīntiān jiǔ yuè sān hào.
今天9月3号。

F. Jīntiān xīngqī jǐ?
今天星期几？

**6** 中国人、英国人、美国人写的日期有什么不同？What differences are there between how dates are written in China, Britain and the US?

**7** 做一张今年你的生日的日历。Make a calendar page in Chinese for your birthday this year.

# Lesson 10 现在几点？
## What time is it?

**1** 老师读数字，学生快速圈出来。 Students circle the numbers the teacher reads out as fast as they can.

| 1 | 2 | 3 | 4 | 5 | 6 | 7 | 8 | 9 | 10 |
|---|---|---|---|---|---|---|---|---|---|
| 11 | 12 | 13 | 14 | 15 | 16 | 17 | 18 | 19 | 20 |
| 21 | 22 | 23 | 24 | 25 | 26 | 27 | 28 | 29 | 30 |
| 31 | 32 | 33 | 34 | 35 | 36 | 37 | 38 | 39 | 40 |
| 41 | 42 | 43 | 44 | 45 | 46 | 47 | 48 | 49 | 50 |
| 51 | 52 | 53 | 54 | 55 | 56 | 57 | 58 | 59 | 60 |

**2** 两人一组，一人说时间，另一人在空表盘上画出时针和分针。 In pairs, one student says a time in the table and the other draws the corresponding hour and minute hands on one of the clock faces.

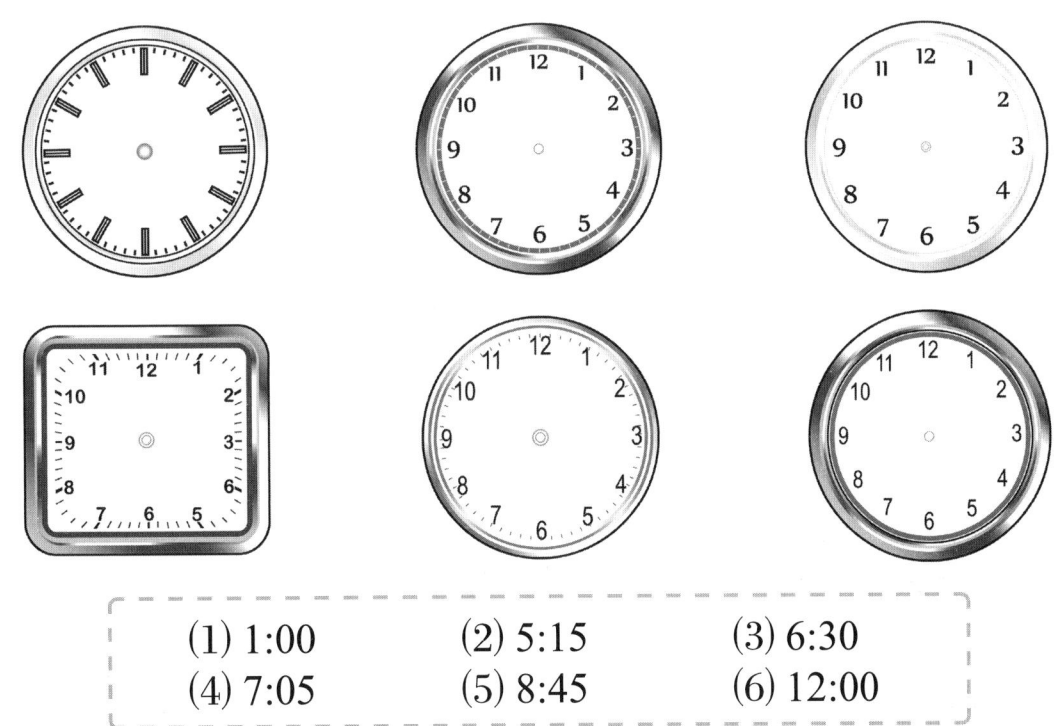

(1) 1:00   (2) 5:15   (3) 6:30
(4) 7:05   (5) 8:45   (6) 12:00

37

**3** 扔橡皮。Throw the eraser.

两人轮流扔橡皮，橡皮落在哪个格子里，就用哪个时间回答问题。In pairs, students take it in turns to throw an eraser onto the grid below. One then asks question A, and the other replies using the time in the box which the eraser landed on.

例：A：Xiànzài jǐ diǎn? 现在几点？
　　B：Xiànzài 现在_____。

| wǔ diǎn 五点 | sān diǎn shí fēn 三点十分 | shí'èr diǎn 十二点 |
|---|---|---|
| qī diǎn shí'èr 七点十二 | liù diǎn 六点 | yī diǎn shíwǔ 一点十五 |
| sì diǎn shíbā 四点十八 | sān diǎn wǔshí 三点五十 | qī diǎn 七点 |
| bā diǎn 八点 | jiǔ diǎn sānshí 九点三十 | shíyī diǎn 十一点 |
| shíyī diǎn shí fēn 十一点十分 | sān diǎn sìshíwǔ 三点四十五 | bā diǎn wǔshíjiǔ 八点五十九 |

现在几点？
What time is it?

10

④ **做时钟。** Make a clock.

★ 描一描表盘上的汉字数字。
Trace over the characters of numbers on the clock face.

★ 剪下表盘、时针和分针。
Cut out the clock face, the hour and minute hands.

★ 把时针和分针钉在表盘上。
Pin the hands onto the clock face.

★ 涂上自己喜欢的颜色。
Color in the clock using your favorite colors.

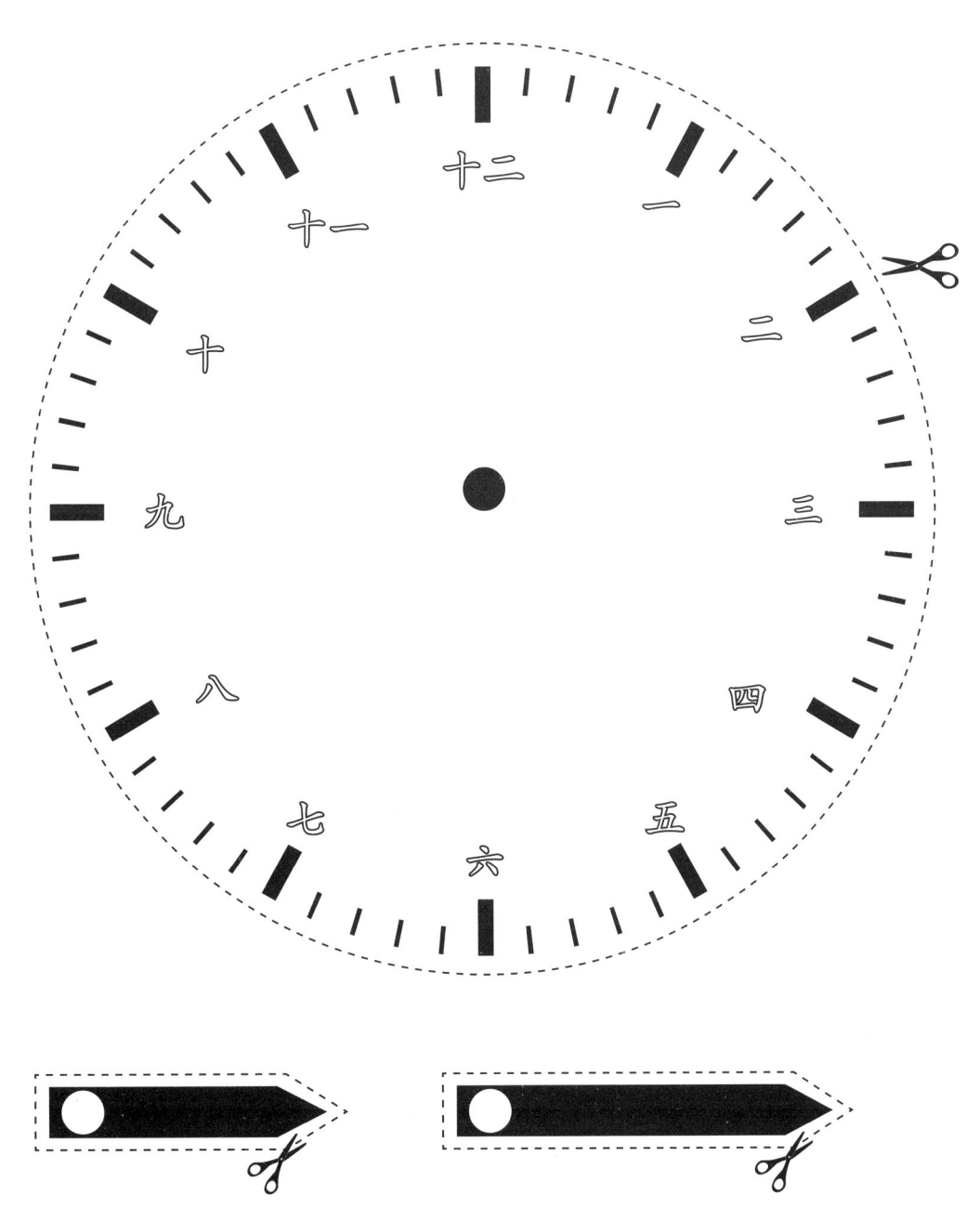

**5** 我的小书：我的一天。 My Chinese diary: A day in my life.

---

Wǒ de xiǎo shū: wǒ de yì tiān
我的小书：我的一天

Míngzi
名字（name）：_____

---

Wǒ zǎoshang ___ diǎn ___ fēn qǐchuáng.
我早上____点____分起床
（get up）。

---

Wǒ zǎoshang ___ diǎn ___ fēn qù xuéxiào.
我早上____点____分去学校。

---

Wǒ zhōngwǔ ___ diǎn ___ fēn chīfàn.
我中午____点____分吃饭
（have lunch）。

---

Wǒ xiàwǔ ___ diǎn ___ fēn fàngxué.
我下午____点____分放学
（leave school）。

---

Wǒ xiàwǔ ___ diǎn ___ fēn huíjiā.
我下午____点____分回家
（go back home）。

---

Wǒ wǎnshang ___ diǎn ___ fēn chī wǎnfàn.
我晚上____点____分吃晚饭
（do homework）。

---

Wǒ wǎnshang ___ diǎn ___ fēn shuìjiào.
我晚上____点____分睡觉
（go to sleep）。

# Lesson 11 你吃什么？
## What would you like to eat?

**1** 描一描，写一写。 Trace the characters and write them.

 niú：cow, cattle

牛 牛 牛
ノ 亠 二 牛

 mǐ：rice

米 米 米
丶 ⼃ 二 半 米 米

 shuǐ：water

水 水 水
丨 ⼓ 才 水

**2** 找一找，圈一圈。 Find and circle the *Pinyin* for the Chinese words below.

| chī | wǒ | píng | nǎ | hē |
|---|---|---|---|---|
| miàn | tiáo | guǒ | tā | dàn |
| niú | nǎi | xǐ | huan | gāo |
| qù | shàng | mǐ | fàn | dà |
| jiā | diàn | shuí | gāo | shuǐ |

píngguǒ
苹果（apple）

miàntiáo
面条（noodles）

mǐfàn
米饭（rice）

niúnǎi
牛奶（milk）

dàngāo
蛋糕（cake）

shuǐ
水（water）

**3** 猜一猜，连一连。Guess the meanings of the following words and match them with the pictures.

**4** 读一读，找不同。Read and find the different one in each group.

| | | | | |
|---|---|---|---|---|
| 例： | A. wǒ 我 | B. nǐ 你 | C. tā 他 | D. chī 吃 (圈) |
| (1) | A. miàntiáo 面条 | B. mǐfàn 米饭 | C. shāngdiàn 商店 | D. dàngāo 蛋糕 |
| (2) | A. xǐhuan 喜欢 | B. yǎnjing 眼睛 | C. bízi 鼻子 | D. ěrduo 耳朵 |
| (3) | A. niǎo 鸟 | B. yú 鱼 | C. māo 猫 | D. shuǐ 水 |
| (4) | A. dà 大 | B. cháng 长 | C. gāo 高 | D. chī 吃 |
| (5) | A. kàn 看 | B. bù 不 | C. qù 去 | D. hē 喝 |

你吃什么？
What would you like to eat?

11

**5** 找一找，涂一涂。Find and color in the items on Susan's shopping list.

Susan's shopping list

| yú | shuǐ | niúnǎi | miàntiáo | dàngāo | bǐsà |
|---|---|---|---|---|---|
| 鱼 | 水 | 牛奶 | 面条 | 蛋糕 | 比萨 |

**6** 看一看，说一说。Have conversations with your partner using the pictures to guide you.

(1)

(2)

(3)

(4)

Word box

| hé | chī | shénme | xǐhuan |
|---|---|---|---|
| 和 | 吃 | 什么 | 喜欢 |

43

**7** 画一画，说一说。Draw what you had for lunch today, and describe it to your partner in Chinese.

例：    Jīntiān wǒ chī           hē
　　今天我吃_____，喝_____。

**8** 和父母一起做。Work with your parents to make a list of kinds of food you have and don't have in your house. Then write them down here in *Pinyin* or Chinese characters.

Wǒ jiā yǒu ...
我家有……

(1)

(2)

(3)

(4)

(5)

Wǒ jiā méiyǒu ...
我家没有……

(1)

(2)

(3)

(4)

(5)

# 参考答案 Answers

### Lesson 2　你叫什么?

② (1) rènshi, to know
　 (2) shénme, what
③ (1) C　(2) A　(3) B
④ (1) A　(2) B　(3) B　(4) A

### Lesson 3　他是谁?

⑥ (1) B　(2) D　(3) E, C　(4) A

### Lesson 4　我家有四口人。

① 爸爸3个，妈妈4个，哥哥2个，姐姐3个，妹妹1个
② bàba, māma, gēge, jiějie, mèimei, wǒ

### Lesson 5　我6岁。

① (1) C　(2) E　(3) D　(4) B　(5) A
③ (1) 8　(2) 10　(3) 15　(4) 23　(5) 一
　 (6) 三　(7) 二十　(8) 八十一
④ (1) 三　(2) 一　(3) 九　(4) 十

### Lesson 7　这是谁的狗?

① (1) A　(2) B　(3) C　(4) B

### Lesson 9　今天星期几?

② (1) 天　(2) 几　(3) 小鸟　(4) 喜欢
③ (1) 4, 5　(2) 10, 11
　 (3) 14, 2, 15　(4) 天, 一
⑤ (1) D　(2) F　(3) C　(4) D　(5) A
　 (6) B

### Lesson 11　你吃什么?

④ (1) C　(2) A　(3) D　(4) D　(5) B

## 郑重声明

高等教育出版社依法对本书享有专有出版权。任何未经许可的复制、销售行为均违反《中华人民共和国著作权法》，其行为人将承担相应的民事责任和行政责任；构成犯罪的，将被依法追究刑事责任。为了维护市场秩序，保护读者的合法权益，避免读者误用盗版书造成不良后果，我社将配合行政执法部门和司法机关对违法犯罪的单位和个人进行严厉打击。社会各界人士如发现上述侵权行为，希望及时举报，我社将奖励举报有功人员。

反盗版举报电话　（010）58581999　58582371
反盗版举报邮箱　dd@hep.com.cn
通信地址　北京市西城区德外大街4号　高等教育出版社法律事务部
邮政编码　100120

读者意见反馈

为收集对教材的意见建议，进一步完善教材编写并做好服务工作，读者可将对本教材的意见建议通过如下渠道反馈至我社。

咨询电话　400-810-0598
反馈邮箱　wy_dzyj@pub.hep.cn
通信地址　北京市朝阳区惠新东街4号富盛大厦1座
　　　　　高等教育出版社总编辑办公室
邮政编码　100029

### 图书在版编目（CIP）数据

YCT标准教程活动手册. 1 / 苏英霞主编; 王蕾, 蔡楠编. -- 北京 : 高等教育出版社, 2017.12（2024.11重印）
ISBN 978-7-04-048217-1

Ⅰ. ①Y… Ⅱ. ①苏… ②王… ③蔡… Ⅲ. ①汉语 – 对外汉语教学 – 水平考试 – 教学参考资料 Ⅳ. ①H195.4

中国版本图书馆CIP数据核字 (2017) 第231252号

| | | | | | | | |
|---|---|---|---|---|---|---|---|
| 策划编辑 | 梁　宇 | 责任编辑 | 李　玮 | 封面设计 | 冰河文化 | 版式设计 | 冰河文化 |
| 插图绘制 | 冰河文化 | 责任校对 | 杨　曦 | 责任印制 | 刘弘远 | | |

| | | | | |
|---|---|---|---|---|
| 出版发行 | 高等教育出版社 | 网　　址 | http://www.hep.edu.cn | |
| 社　　址 | 北京市西城区德外大街4号 | | http://www.hep.com.cn | |
| 邮政编码 | 100120 | 网上订购 | http://www.hepmall.com.cn | |
| 印　　刷 | 天津鑫丰华印务有限公司 | | http://www.hepmall.com | |
| 开　　本 | 889mm×1194mm 1/16 | | http://www.hepmall.cn | |
| 印　　张 | 3.25 | 版　　次 | 2017年12月第1版 | |
| 字　　数 | 50千字 | 印　　次 | 2024年11月第13次印刷 | |
| 购书热线 | 010-58581118 | 定　　价 | 25.00元 | |
| 咨询电话 | 400-810-0598 | | | |

本书如有缺页、倒页、脱页等质量问题，请到所购图书销售部门联系调换
版权所有　侵权必究
物 料 号　48217-00